T0052739

Since 1888, *National Geographic* magazine has provided its readers a wealth of information and helped us understand the world in which we live. Insightful articles, supported by gorgeous photography and impeccable research, bring the mission of the National Geographic Society front and center: to inspire people to care about the planet. The *Explore* series delivers *National Geographic* to you in the same spirit. Each of the books in this series presents the best articles on popular and relevant topics in an accessible format. In addition, each book highlights the work of National Geographic Explorers, photographers, and writers. Explore the world of *National Geographic*. You will be inspired.

ON THE COVER
Windswept dunes and salty lakes of the Badain Jaran dune field in the Gobi

Genghis Khan and the Gobi

Mongolian falcon spreading its wings

Much of the Gobi, a desert that stretches across parts of China and Mongolia, is a barren, harsh landscape with little sign of human life. The people who do inhabit this area often live as their ancestors did centuries ago. Although life for them is changing, many still move from place to place in search of food for their herds, preserving their traditions and celebrating the heroes of the past.

Mongolia and the Gobi have a rich and often glorious past. Nearly a thousand years ago, trade routes called the Silk Roads crossed the desert and mountains of the Gobi. Along these roads, merchant caravans carried goods and knowledge from east to west. The Silk Roads changed history. So did the empire Genghis Khan established and expanded thousands of miles across the known world, with Mongolia at its center.

Going back even farther in time, the Gobi is the site of archaeological treasures as well as prehistoric finds that date from the age of the dinosaurs. Mongolia is one of the few places left in the world where scientists can find dinosaur fossils where they originally came to rest.

In this book you will find articles about Mongolia and the Gobi adapted from *National Geographic*. The stories and photos they contain will help you explore the region's past and present. You'll learn about the Gobi's varied terrain and meet modern Mongolians who struggle to find a place in a changing world. You'll read the story of Mongolia's national hero Genghis Khan, who started his life in this parched land and went on to make his mark on the world. You'll also meet a National Geographic Explorer who is intent on finding Genghis's lost tomb. He describes the excitement of working in the field and the importance of protecting Mongolia's priceless heritage. After reading these articles, you may agree that the Gobi's riches are worth more than money or gold and well worth preserving for the future.

MONGOLIAN FALCONER
A falconer—a person who trains birds of prey—and his golden eagle hunt on horseback in Mongolia.

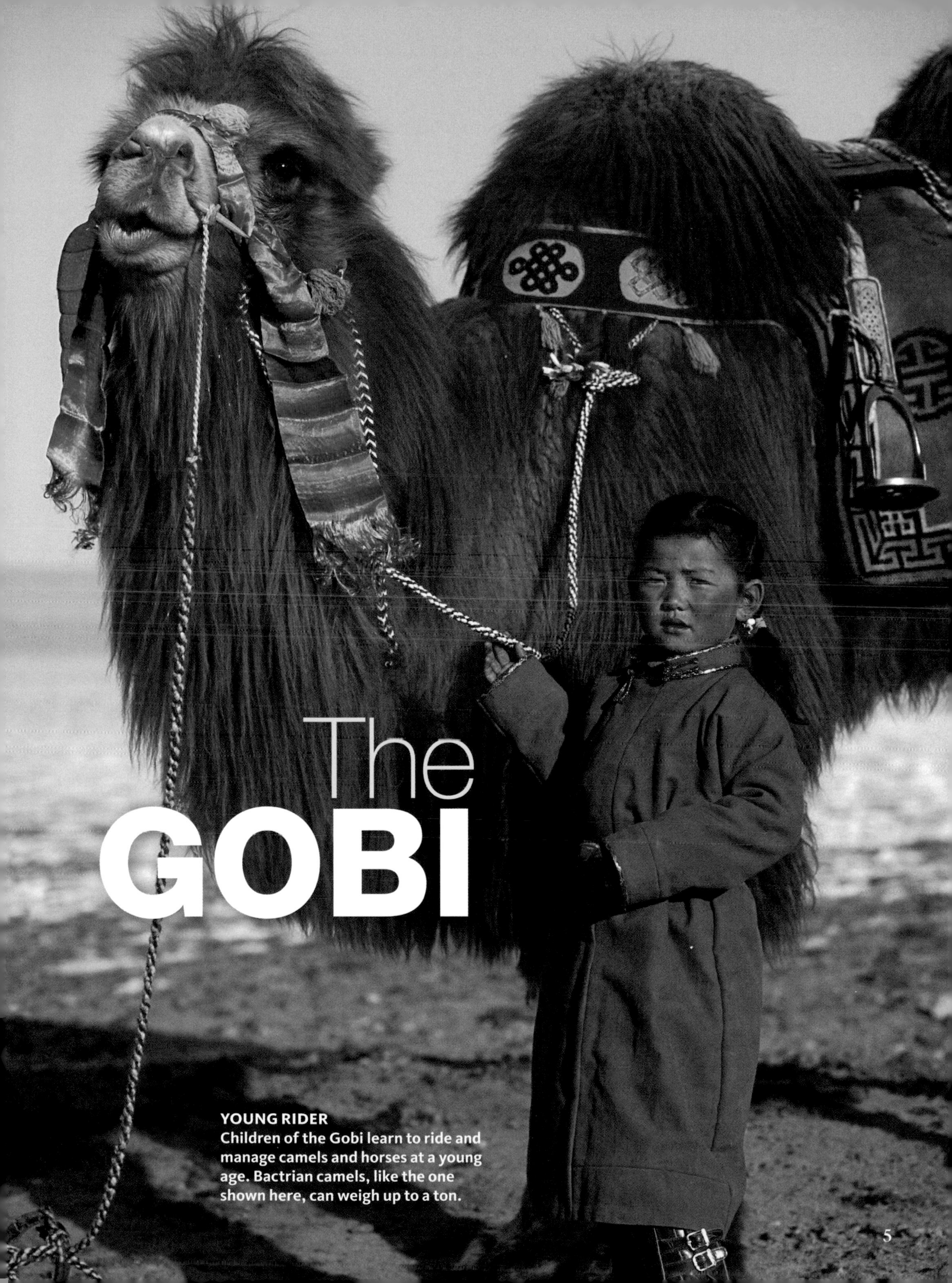

The
GOBI

YOUNG RIDER
Children of the Gobi learn to ride and manage camels and horses at a young age. Bactrian camels, like the one shown here, can weigh up to a ton.

SUMMER IN THE GOBI

The contrast between seasons in the Gobi can be extreme. Summer temperatures at the Khongor sand dunes (shown below) in southern Mongolia can rise above 100°F in the summer months.

WINTER IN THE GOBI

During the winter, temperatures can plunge well below zero as icy winds blow. The dunes receive very little precipitation, but some snow does build up.

WILD HORSE HERDER
A Mongolian herdsman tries to catch a horse in the foothills of the Khangai Mountains. Wild horse populations in the Gobi have recently been increasing in size since their near extinction in the late 1960s.

HOME ON THE STEPPE
A Mongolian family poses in front of their ger. Among Mongolian nomads, it is common for several generations to live under one roof.

LIFE AND REGIONS OF THE GOBI

The Gobi is a land of extremes: monster sand dunes, exposed bare rock, jagged mountains, high **plateaus**, and deep valleys. It covers 500,000 square miles in southern Mongolia and northern and northwestern China.

The region is commonly referred to as a "desert." Technically, though, it is a mixture of desert and semi-desert. Winter temperatures can plunge to 40 degrees below zero. Summer temperatures can soar to 122°F. Some days, the temperature can change as much as 95 degrees.

Not surprisingly, the Gobi is one of the least populated places on Earth. Still, tens of thousands of nomadic herders live in this difficult land. Families set up camp with their horses, small flocks of sheep and herds of goats, camels, and cows. When the animals have depleted the nearby grasses, the families pack up and move to another location. To find enough grazing land, families may move several times a year.

Nomadic families live in **gers** (also called yurts), or portable structures that can be assembled in less than an hour. Gers are constructed on circular wooden frames, which are covered in thick felt. Inside are rugs, beds, storage chests, and stoves fueled by wood or dung (animal waste).

The Gobi is made up of five regions. Each region has a distinct climate, topography, wildlife, and vegetation.

The ❶ **Eastern Gobi Desert Steppe** is a treeless plain. Its drought-resistant shrubs and grasses survive on only four to six inches of rain a year. The **steppe** features flat, dry grasslands as well as desert basins with salt pans and ponds.

The ❷ **Alashan Plateau** is the largest of the regions. It is bounded by high mountains, interspersed with low-lying oases, and marked by hundreds of miles of waterless clay and sand. The plateau has diverse wildlife, including the Bactrian camel.

The ❸ **Gobi Lakes Valley** is a long narrow area bordered by mountain ranges. Marshes and

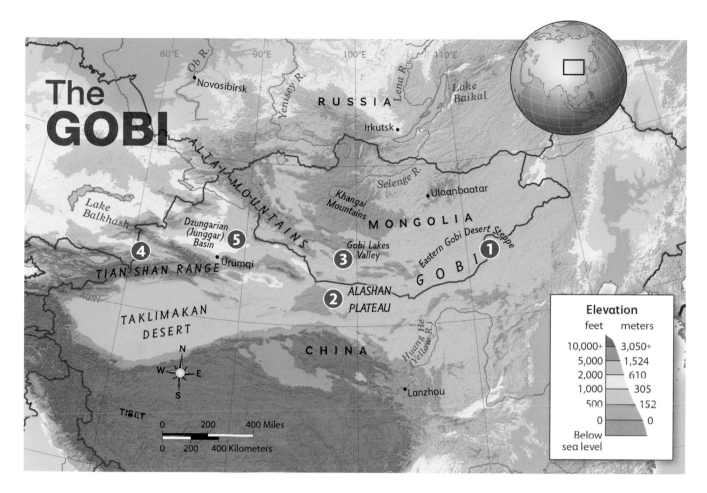

The Gobi

Elevation

feet	meters
10,000+	3,050+
5,000	1,524
2,000	610
1,000	305
500	152
0	0
Below sea level	

lakes are fed by run-off from the mountains and then dry up for part of the year. The birds, amphibians, and reptiles here are adapted to both arid and wet conditions.

The higher elevations of the ❹ **Tian Shan Range** receive nearly four times the amount of precipitation than most of the Gobi. Melting snow feeds rivers and streams. Fruit trees grow in the lower mountain areas.

The ❺ **Dzungarian Basin** is surrounded by mountains. Much of this area is desert, receiving only 6 to 12 inches of precipitation a year. The basin also has steppes that receive water from mountain streams in the spring.

THINK ABOUT IT!

1 **Interpret Maps** Use the map of the Gobi to write two additional facts about the location and topography of each region.

2 **Describe Geographic Information** Compare and contrast the geographic information you have learned about the Gobi with the region where you live.

3 **Draw Conclusions** Which region of the Gobi has the highest elevation? Use the map legend and the text to determine your answer.

BACKGROUND & VOCABULARY

ger *n.* (GUR) a round building that is easy to assemble; the traditional home of Mongolian nomads; also called yurts

plateau *n.* (pla-TOH) an area of level land at a high elevation

steppe *n.* (STEP) dry, usually level, largely grass-covered land in regions of wide temperature range

The Million-Dollar DINOSAUR

Tarbosaurus bataar—which means "alarming lizard"—was a dinosaur that lived almost exclusively in Mongolia about 65 million years ago. Paleontologists have studied the fossils of Tarbosaurus and have a good idea of what this dinosaur may have looked like. Check out this illustration of a Tarbosaurus.

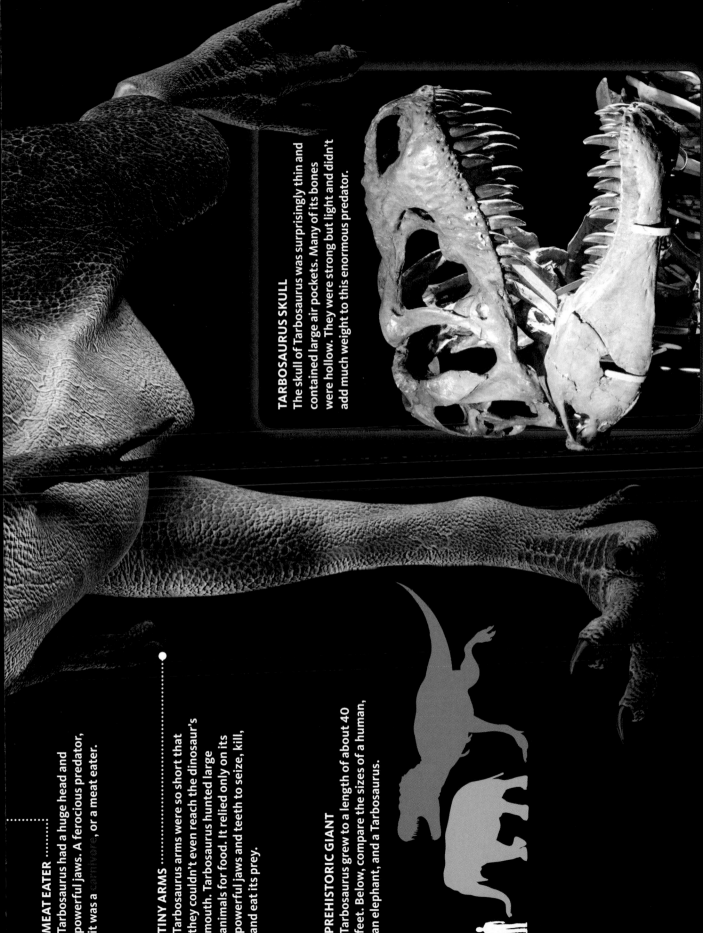

MEAT EATER

Tarbosaurus had a huge head and powerful jaws. A ferocious predator, it was a carnivore, or a meat eater.

TINY ARMS

Tarbosaurus arms were so short that they couldn't even reach the dinosaur's mouth. Tarbosaurus hunted large animals for food. It relied only on its powerful jaws and teeth to seize, kill, and eat its prey.

PREHISTORIC GIANT

Tarbosaurus grew to a length of about 40 feet. Below, compare the sizes of a human, an elephant, and a Tarbosaurus.

TARBOSAURUS SKULL

The skull of Tarbosaurus was surprisingly thin and contained large air pockets. Many of its bones were hollow. They were strong but light and didn't add much weight to this enormous predator.

THE ILLEGAL FOSSIL TRADE

Paleontologists and other scientists **excavate** and preserve dinosaur fossils. Sometimes, though, wind and water expose fossils that have been covered by rock. Once the fossils are uncovered, those same forces of wind and water begin to break them down, so the race is on to study them before they disappear. In Mongolia alone, there are 89 sites where Tarbosaurus skeletons have been excavated, and the number is growing.

In order to understand a species, scientists need to be able to compare and contrast multiple **specimens** of that species. A fossil of an immature Tarbosaurus, for example, helps paleontologists understand how the dinosaurs grew. A group of adult fossils can tell how much the full-grown animals varied in size. The more specimens scientists can study, the more complete a picture they can draw.

Paleontologists are therefore rightly concerned about the practices of professional fossil dealers. Some of these **commercial** collectors are expert fossil hunters themselves. They excavate the specimens and prepare them for scientific study or exhibition. Most fossil dealers obey the law and earn an honest living. But then there are those who don't. Criminals make millions by **smuggling,** or illegally exporting and selling fossils, and the harm they do cannot be measured. These fossils often end up in private collections, rather than in institutions where they can be studied.

In addition, fossil thieves destroy information found in the rocks around the fossils. They also fail to record the positions in which fossil bones are found. The rocks can help paleontologists figure out the age of a fossil. The position of the bones can help scientists figure out how a dinosaur died and what happened to its body after death. This is called "geologic context."

In many cases, illegal excavators damage the specimens themselves in the process of digging them up. Sometimes they are deliberately destroyed to remove valuable parts that are easily transported and sold. One Tarbosaurus tooth, for example, might fetch as much as $16,000 when auctioned alone.

THE MILLION-DOLLAR DINOSAUR

One of the most famous cases of fossil theft in recent years involved a nearly complete *Tarbosaurus bataar* skeleton. This dinosaur was up for auction in the United States, where it would likely become part of a private collection.

Paleontologists were certain that the dinosaur came from Mongolia, the only place in the world where Tarbosaurus skeletons are found in great numbers. Experts agreed that there was no way the fossilized skeleton could have left Mongolia legally. The Mongolian government decides who is allowed to excavate dinosaurs and where the fossils can be displayed. There was no sign that the Mongolian government had approved the excavation of this particular Tarbosaurus.

Days before the auction, paleontologists, the president of Mongolia, and lawyers working with the Mongolian government demanded that the sale be stopped. The auction house went ahead anyway. The final selling price of the Tarbosaurus was just over $1 million. But the sale could not be finalized until the legal status of the skeleton had been settled.

Mongolian and international paleontologists were called in to check the specimen. They confirmed that the Tarbosaurus must have been uncovered in Mongolia. Moreover, they discovered that the skeleton was actually made up of pieces from several different dinosaurs.

Investigators also learned that the bones had been shipped from Great Britain to the United States as "assorted reptile fossils." A month later the U.S. government seized the skeleton and declared it to be smuggled goods.

The saga of the Tarbosaurus skeleton captured Mongolians' attention, and the story became a major media event. A Mongolian paleontologist who consulted on the case commented, "It is not only on the news; just talking to the people in Mongolia, they really want to know what is going on with the whole case."

Frustratingly, the trend of looting dinosaur bones seems to be on the rise. Thieves have been taking fossils from Mongolia's approved dig sites, causing damage to the legal excavations

FOSSIL PRIDE
Mongolians take great pride in displaying the fossils of their dinosaurs, including this Tarbosaurus at a museum in Ulaanbataar.

and potentially destroying important scientific information. The Mongolian government, with the enthusiastic support of the scientific community, is trying to stem the tide of illegal fossil hunting.

The bones of the million-dollar dinosaur ended up back in Mongolia. The thief might be sent to prison for smuggling. But will Mongolia continue to lose its precious dinosaur fossils at such a rate? Only time will tell.

THINK ABOUT IT! ||||||||||||||||||||||||||||

1 **Synthesize** What characteristics of the Tarbosaurus might have made it an "alarming lizard" to other animals?

2 **Make Inferences** Paleontologists from all over the world come to Mongolia to work. What attracts them to this area?

3 **Analyze Cause and Effect** What harm do illegal fossil collectors cause? Explain the effects of this illegal activity.

BACKGROUND & VOCABULARY

carnivore *n.* (kahr-nih-VOHR) an animal that eats meat

commercial *adj.* (kuh-MUR-shuhl) having to do with business; for profit

excavate *v.* (EHX-kuh-vayt) to dig to uncover buried items

smuggle *v.* (SMUH-guhl) to transport items illegally from one country to another

specimen *n.* (SPEH-suh-mehn) an individual plant or animal that can serve as an example of the group to which it belongs

A CONQUEROR'S FACE
This bronze plaque depicts the face of the Mongol emperor Genghis Khan.

16

LORD
OF THE
MONGOLS

Adapted from "Lord of the Mongols," by Mike Edwards,
in *National Geographic*, December 1996

*Respected founder of Mongolia, this ruthless 13th-century
warrior launched an empire that reached as far as Europe.*

FIERCE WARRIOR

Samarkand, Bukhara, Urgench, Merv, Herat.
One after another the rich cities of Central Asia
toppled before the horsemen bursting from
the steppe of Mongolia. Rarely had the world
witnessed such a whirlwind of destruction. In the
words of one Persian historian, the Mongolian
cavalry was "more numerous than ants or
locusts" and more plentiful than the "sand of
the desert or drops of rain." Imagine the scene:
tens of thousands of riders on horses and camels,
trailed by a great herd of spare mounts, and in
front thousands of civilians, a human shield.

Never had an empire expanded so quickly,
across such distances. At its height, Mongol rule
stretched all the way from China in the east to
the Mediterranean in the west.

Genghis Khan, fierce warrior and respected
father of his country, launched this brutal
campaign and, in the process, transformed a
poor, sparsely populated land in the parched
Gobi desert into the center of one of the greatest
empires of all time.

The question usually asked about the Mongols
is, "Were they simply robbers and killers?" Not
in Mongolian eyes. To the Mongolians, Genghis

Khan was the country's George Washington, a
unifier of his people. During campaigns both
east and west, he and his Mongol army captured
scholars, physicians, artisans, architects, and
government officials. They brought them all back
to Mongolia to build, to educate, and to organize
a functioning government for the empire.

Even as a military leader, Genghis didn't
always choose slaughter and destruction. Some
cities that offered no resistance escaped with
payment of riches to the invader and looting by
Genghis's army—standard practices for the time.
Many rulers chose to collaborate rather than be
wiped out. From their kingdoms, the Mongols
drew not only taxes but also troops, swelling
the ranks of Genghis's fighting force. To their
credit, the Mongols were tolerant of the religions
practiced in conquered cities. In Genghis's own
clan were Buddhists, Muslims, and Christians as
well as worshippers of traditional gods.

Nevertheless the Mongols did ruthlessly kill
both opposing armies and innocent victims, and
they **subjugated** millions as they pursued their
dream of empire. The 13th century was one of
the most war torn in history, and Genghis was a
man of his time.

BECOMING KHAN

Much of what is known about Genghis Khan comes from an ancient book called *The Secret History of the Mongols*, a source filled with myths and legends as well as historical information. The *Secret History* relates that Genghis was born by the Onon River, some 200 miles northeast of Ulaanbaatar, and named Temujin (tay-MOO-jihn), meaning "blacksmith." At that time, in the 1160s, Mongolia was a realm of perhaps 30 **nomadic** tribes, with a total population between 1.5 million and 3 million.

The *Secret History* offers a wealth of detail on Temujin's rise to power. At first, life was difficult. When Temujin was nine, his father was poisoned by Tatar tribesmen. As a young man Temujin made allies. One was Jamuqa, who became his *anda*, or blood brother. Another was Toghril, a leader of another tribe. When Temujin's bride was kidnapped in a raid, these friends mustered warriors to rescue her.

As an adult, Temujin gradually brought several tribes under his control by conquest or by bestowing gifts. In dealing with the Tatars, who killed his father, he was merciless. All but the youngest males were killed, and children and women were enslaved. Because of Temujin's revenge, the Tatar tribe ceased to exist.

As Temujin's influence increased, alliances shifted. His friends Jamuqa and Toghril opposed his growing power. In response, Temujin crushed Toghril's army in a fierce three-day clash. Then, in 1205, he defeated his last powerful enemy. Fighting on the enemy's side was Jamuqa, who was captured. "Let me die quickly," he asked. Temujin granted his blood brother's wish.

In 1206, at a great assembly of tribes, Temujin was enthroned as Genghis Khan—"strong ruler" or perhaps "oceanic ruler," hence ruler of the world. He was about 40 years old.

Soon after Genghis became the great khan, the Mongol army was on the move. Genghis's first campaign beyond Mongolia was in 1209 against the kingdom of Xi Xia (shee shee-AH). To reach the capital, the Mongols had to cross the forbidding Gobi desert. Such travel was no great obstacle to nomads who, in a pinch, could live on mare's milk and blood drawn from a slit in a horse's hide.

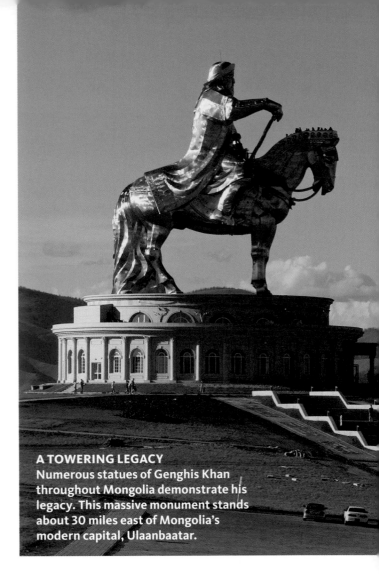

A TOWERING LEGACY
Numerous statues of Genghis Khan throughout Mongolia demonstrate his legacy. This massive monument stands about 30 miles east of Mongolia's modern capital, Ulaanbaatar.

Ruled by a Tibetan people, Xi Xia produced fine cloth and controlled watering holes along the important trade route known as the Silk Road. The kingdom charged heavy taxes from traders, including Mongol traders.

Genghis was already molding his army into the disciplined force that would ride into Europe and deep into China. He organized his troops on a decimal system: a squad of 10, a company of 100, a division of 10,000. Moreover, he erased tribal structures within the army. Tribes were scattered among various units, and command went to proven warriors, not tribal chiefs.

When Genghis came against the Xi Xia army in a mountain pass and could not break through, he **feigned** withdrawal, a favorite Mongol trick. The enemy came out in pursuit. Suddenly the Mongols turned, shooting arrows at a speed of six per minute and capturing the Xi Xia commander. The emperor sought peace in 1210 and pledged loyalty to Genghis Khan.

CONQUERING THE JIN

Genghis Khan then turned his eyes upon the kingdom east of Xi Xia, which had at least 20 million people and was vastly richer. In Genghis's era, this kingdom was ruled by people known as the Jurchen, who called their **dynasty** Jin, or "golden." Like dynasties before, the Jin paid tribute to the nomads and traded luxury goods, grain, and tools for the nomads' animals and hides. Terms were generous, a kind of bribe paid to protect against raids.

But the Jin had fallen on hard times, and Genghis had learned from Jin merchants that the riches were drying up. Genghis knew, too, that much of the huge Jin army was occupied in the south. Thus Genghis was taking aim at a weakened government.

In 1211 the Mongol army set out, 70,000 strong. Genghis easily broke through the Jins' protective walls. Chinese accounts say that

frustrated frontier troops even deserted and joined the Mongol forces. But many battles lay ahead. Elite Jin troops waited in the Juyong Pass to intercept the Mongols, who were heading to the capital. One of Genghis's trusted generals, Jebe, who was nicknamed "Arrow," caught the defenders off guard by using the feigned retreat trick.

Genghis did not march immediately on the capital. His horsemen were good with the bow, able to shoot forward or backward at full gallop, but he lacked the means to attack the capital's 40-foot walls. Instead, Genghis sent his troops to ravage the countryside.

When at last he surrounded the capital in 1214, Genghis had acquired Chinese catapults that could hurl 100-pound stones against walls and gates. These were not needed, however. Beset with problems, the Jin emperor offered gold, silver, and other treasure if the Mongols would withdraw.

CENTER OF THE EMPIRE
A stone tortoise is one of the few ruins of Karakorum, the 13th-century Mongol capital. Stones from the ruins were later used to build a 16th-century monastery, shown in the background.

The Jin emperor moved his capital south, and Genghis suspected him of regrouping to attack. The Mongols stormed back to the original capital in 1215 to starve the city into submission and massacre its people. Genghis carried off massive amounts of treasure the emperor had left behind.

Returning to Mongolia, Genghis began to think of building a capital. From Xi Xia he had claimed 30,000 artisans, some of whom may have helped build the city of Karakorum. Perhaps Genghis intended Karakorum to become a monumental city such as those that had been built by the Chinese. It never achieved such greatness, although it had huge palaces as well as a treasury, a mosque, a Buddhist temple, and probably a Christian church.

Genghis got a scholar in China to advise him on building a government. He recruited accountants and scribes from conquered territory. Soon a school was turning out Mongol administrators, tax collectors, and record keepers.

TROUBLE IN THE WEST

Meanwhile, Genghis was troubled by events at Mongolia's western edge. Kuchlug, a Mongolian prince, had seized power and was gathering other allies. In 1218 General Jebe attacked Kuchlug's forces with 20,000 horsemen.

Most of the people in the region were Muslims. Kuchlug had forbidden them to worship and had even executed a Muslim spiritual leader. When Jebe appeared, there was rejoicing—a rare reception for the dreaded Mongols. Kuchlug was beheaded, and Genghis took the grateful people under his wing.

Now that his realm touched the Khwarizm empire, Genghis sent an array of gifts to its leader, Shah Muhammad: jade, ivory, gold, cloaks of white camel wool. Genghis also proposed trade and sent out a caravan of 450 merchants.

They only reached Utrar on the eastern edge of Muhammad's realm. The governor there

attacked farther south. Genghis rode west to the city of Bukhara. Muhammad had no strategy other than to keep his troops hunkered down in his cities.

Utrar held out for a month or longer, as boulders rained down and rooftops were bombed with a flammable mixture called naphtha. The governor who had slain Genghis's merchants fought to the end, flinging bricks from the top of the fortress. The victorious Mongols leveled the fortress and the city walls.

At Bukhara, the city fathers opened the gates, and Genghis rode into the courtyard of the immense mosque. Bahadur Kozakov, curator of Bukhara's museum, described the scene.

"He [Genghis] had all the musicians of the city summoned. Genghis listened to the music. But he wasn't just having a party. He ordered the nobility brought to him with their riches. When their gold and stones were at his feet, he gave the city to his troops to rob. The nomads loved to rob cities. The mosque was burned, and the fire probably spread. It was complete disorder," describes Kozakov.

The Mongol **hordes** rampaged on. Following a fierce battle, they toppled Urgench, a great Silk Road city. There, after slaying 100,000 defenders, they mercilessly diverted a river to flood the city's ruins.

The Mongols moved south to the city of Merv. According to one historian, a Muslim holy man and his helpers spent 13 days counting corpses in the rubble of Merv, tallying 1.3 million. One city in Afghanistan did not resist, but its citizens were massacred anyway.

Were these tales of wholesale slaughter completely accurate? Some cities were surely destroyed to be an example to others. But not all cities met that fate. And the numbers of victims were most likely exaggerated.

Genghis destroyed enemy armies certainly, and many civilians probably died during sieges or as they were marched in front of the armies as the first line of defense.

But the Mongols needed defeated civilians to move their pack trains and siege weapons. Moreover, they were an army on the move with little time to methodically line up and kill hundreds of thousands of people.

suspected that they were spies. Indeed, some probably were. So he seized and executed the Mongol merchants.

Genghis sent an ambassador to demand that the shah hand over the governor for punishment. Muhammad killed the ambassador and sent his head to Genghis. The Mongols viewed this act as an unforgiveable insult.

No doubt Muhammad felt secure since his army numbered 400,000 men. But many were of uncertain loyalty. Nor did Muhammad enjoy the loyalty of his heavily taxed subjects. Again it was a weakened ruler who braced for a Mongol attack.

Before attacking Khwarizm, Genghis sent a message requesting soldiers from Xi Xia. Back came a tart reply: If Genghis did not have enough troops, he had no business being khan. Genghis would seek revenge for that insult, too.

Though outnumbered by hundreds of thousands, Genghis boldly split his forces. One column besieged the city of Utrar. Another

LARGER THAN LIFE
This illustration from a Persian history of Mongolia, painted in India around 1590, shows Genghis Khan and his army taking a fortress in a northern Chinese province.

MONGOLIAN RIDERS
Mongolia's tradition of skilled riders goes back to Genghis's army. Today, Mongolian boys race horses at annual festivals.

CONQUESTS IN RUSSIA

The Mongols had superior generals. Commanders knew they could depend on their well-disciplined troops. The most important leaders were Genghis's comrades from the tribal wars. Among these, Generals Jebe and Subedei were the finest.

Reaching the Caspian Sea, this bold pair wondered what lay beyond. Europe was unknown to them, so with 20,000 men, they began an exploratory mission. They defeated two armies in Georgia and, crossing the Caucasus Mountains in winter, defeated a coalition of Turkic tribes. Alarm spread through the countryside. In 1223, the Russian princes assembled an army of 80,000 to challenge the Mongols.

Mongol archers on horseback filled the air with arrows. When the princes charged, the archers vanished into the smoke of Mongol fires. The princes discovered that the smoke hid not lightly armored archers but cavalrymen with lances and swords. Parts of the attacking force turned in confusion. They collided with other units, and then a **rout** began.

Jebe and Subedei swept east to the Volga River, fought two more battles, and finally rejoined Genghis on the Central Asian steppe. The army lived off the land, acquired fresh horses by conquest, and defeated every opposing army. In all, they rode 8,000 miles, circling the Caspian Sea in one of the greatest cavalry exploits of all time.

SHARP POINTS
The deadly Mongolian archers used several types of arrow points.

THE LAST CAMPAIGN

Turning for home at last, the Mongols extracted enormous wealth from Central Asia. Warriors blazed with gold chains and jewels, and their horses were laden with bolts of silk and bags of coins. They looted and ravaged cities in their path.

Genghis had not forgotten that the ruler of Xi Xia had refused to supply troops when asked. Moreover, while Genghis was away fighting, Xi Xia had tried to wriggle free of Mongol control. In 1226 the khan led his army south from Mongolia once more.

Several versions exist of Genghis's second Xi Xia campaign. One says that when the Mongols could not get into the capital city, they broke a dike holding back the waters of a canal. The resulting flood undermined the wall, or threatened to, and Xi Xia surrendered. Perhaps Xi Xia surrendered after its army was defeated in fierce battles outside the walls. No one knows for sure.

Whatever happened, it was certain that Genghis Khan was dying. The *Secret History* says that as the Xi Xia campaign began, Genghis went hunting. When his horse shied, he fell, "his body being in great pain." Another account says that Genghis became fatally ill. It is possible he had typhus, a deadly bacterial disease.

From his deathbed Genghis ordered the extermination of the Xi Xia people. His army is said to have killed "mothers and fathers down to the offspring of their offspring." Some were enslaved instead. Still, the destruction of kingdom and people was wholesale.

In August 1227, Genghis Khan died. He was probably 60 years old. Accounts say his body was taken back to Mongolia for burial. To discourage grave robbers, a thousand horsemen are said to have trampled the site until it could not be found. It eludes searchers still.

According to one Persian historian, Genghis was "possessed of great energy, [insight], genius, and understanding, awe-inspiring, a butcher, just, resolute, an overthrower of enemies, intrepid, [bloodthirsty], and cruel." A more complete **epitaph** could not be written, except to add that he left to his clan a unified Mongolia and the most powerful army in the world.

His sons and grandsons sent that army surging into Russia and China, and even farther. Awash in power and wealth, the Mongols would find they had only one dangerous foe: one another. Almost as quickly as the empire rose, it began to fracture into independent domains. Remnants hung on for hundreds of years, but never again would the Gobi desert be the center of a vast and powerful empire.

THINK ABOUT IT! |||||||||||||||||||||||||||||||

1 **Synthesize** Reread the words the Persian historian used to describe Genghis: "possessed of great energy." Choose a positive quality and a negative quality and find examples of these qualities in the article.

2 **Evaluate** Why was Genghis Khan so successful? Give reasons from the article.

3 **Make Inferences** Based on what you have learned about Genghis Khan from this article, what motives do you think drove him to make the choices he did?

BACKGROUND & VOCABULARY

dynasty *n.* (DY-nuh-stee) a series of rulers from the same family

epitaph *n.* (EHP-uh-taf) an inscription in memory of a dead person, as on a tombstone

feign *v.* (FAYN) to pretend

horde *n.* (HORD) a nomadic tribe; a great number

nomadic *adj.* (noh-MAD-ihk) having no fixed residence; moving from place to place

rout *n.* (ROWT) a confused, disorderly retreat

subjugate *v.* (SUHB-juh-gayt) to take control by force; conquer

EXPLORER'S JOURNAL

with Albert Yu-Min Lin

STEPPE RIDER
Taking a break from high-tech archaeology, Albert Lin practices a centuries-old Mongolian sport—horseback riding.

National Geographic Explorer Albert Yu-Min Lin has a dream: to find the lost tomb of Genghis Khan, a goal that has eluded archaeologists and historians for centuries.

FROM PASSION TO PROJECT

When Albert Lin graduated college with a degree in materials science and engineering, his parents urged him to find a steady, well-paying job. Instead, Lin began his career by organizing a high-risk, high-stakes project that offered little stability and even less promise of success.

Lin had been obsessed by the story of Genghis Khan since a backpacking trip to Mongolia. After graduating, he took steps to turn this obsession into action. Some of his best friends at the university were experts in various fields. If combined, Lin believed, their expertise could give a traditional archaeological expedition cutting-edge advantages. Like Lin, his friends were used to roughing it in the wilderness and were up for most any adventure—the crazier the better. They were ready to join him in his Valley of the Khans project. Their destination: Mongolia's most sacred area, Genghis Khan's homeland.

Lin's idea was to use modern digital tools in the field and then to re-create the field sites **virtually** in the lab. The tools he had in mind included digital imaging, computer vision, 3-D mapping, geographic information systems (GIS), and on-site digital archaeology. His goal was to find the sites and then to explore them without disturbing terrain or **artifacts**. This use of technology would preserve the archaeological sites during exploration and help preserve Mongolia's rich cultural heritage.

THE GREAT KHAN

No one is more closely identified with Mongolia's glorious heritage than Genghis Khan: ruler, conqueror, and national hero. For more information about Genghis Khan, read "Lord of the Mongols" on pages 16–25 of this book.

As you may recall, Genghis Khan was born with the name Temujin in the late 12th century. Brilliant, ruthless, and fearless, Temujin forged a mighty army, united Mongolia, and conquered a vast empire spanning much of Asia and Europe.

He was given the title Genghis Khan, which means "strong ruler."

Genghis Khan has captured the imaginations of people worldwide, not just in Mongolia. Albert Lin describes the warriors of Genghis's army: "Ten thousand mounted riders race across a scorching desert, galloping into almost certain death against foes that outnumber them a hundred to one. These riders, ready to die for their new lord, vanquished enemies and unified former rivals under a single banner. In coming together, Mongolia's warring clans formed a hammer that forged the greatest military domination the world has ever seen."

Genghis left his mark on most of the globe. Recently, a large-scale genetic study showed that roughly 16 million people today are his descendants. Yet no portrait exists of the man from his own time. And there are few firsthand written accounts of him.

In August 1227, during a second campaign in China, Genghis died from reasons that remain unknown today. Even less is known about what happened to his body. According to legend,

DRONE TECHNOLOGY
Camera-equipped drones
like this one allow Lin
and his team to explore
the Forbidden Zone, take
photographs, and collect
important information.

all who witnessed the funeral were killed to keep the secret of his tomb's location. Some accounts suggest a large burial near the sacred mountains of his youth. Other historians have speculated that his body lies beneath a river. Still other sources suggest it could be found near his birthplace.

The location of Genghis's tomb remains an enduring mystery. And none of the tombs of the 33 khans who followed Genghis have been found either, although many have searched for them.

THE FORBIDDEN ZONE

The principal goal, the one that inspired Lin's trip, was to find the lost tomb of Genghis Khan. Lin and his Valley of the Khans project teammates focused on an area of Mongolia known as the "Forbidden Zone." The project team's first step was to **survey** the area with GPS, drone flyovers, and satellite imagery.

For nearly 800 years, the Forbidden Zone was as off-limits as any place in the world. Shortly after he died, the Khan's surviving commanders

ordered a group of 50 battle-hardened families to occupy this land and kill any trespassers. The only exceptions were the funeral processions of the Khan's direct descendants. They were allowed to be buried there.

This fierce secrecy led many to believe that the body of Genghis Khan himself lies somewhere in this zone. When the Soviets took over Mongolia in 1924, they stamped out the families in the Forbidden Zone, declared it a military site, and sealed it off from the world. Not until the fall of the Soviet Union in 1991 were restrictions loosened. But even today only a few archaeologists, biologists, and environmentalists have visited the Forbidden Zone.

One early July day, Lin and his team of 18 men found themselves rumbling north in two rented trucks loaded with high-tech mapping and imaging equipment. On maps, their initial destination looked about six hours distant. Then came the mechanical breakdowns and deep mud pits, the injured goats and swamped vehicles. Suspicious guards delayed them at the entrance to the Forbidden Zone. After two days of travel,

the tired expedition members finally established their first base camp.

For the next three weeks they roamed the Forbidden Zone and beyond, crossing the wilderness on foot and on horseback. They braved wolves and avoided unexploded Soviet ammunition. They ate goat steak, goat stew, and something called goat bread, and washed it down with horse milk.

One afternoon, while crossing a valley, Lin spotted a small, rounded grassy hill in the middle of a flat field. It looked like a burial mound, perhaps even a royal mound. The team pushed its way through the thick, boar-infested brush and clambered to the top. A test probe, however, revealed that the hill was just a hill. Their disappointment didn't last long. Two days later, high on the side of a mountain, they arrived at the location of an ancient temple. By simply looking into the upturned earth near recently downed trees, they found plenty of artifacts, including a clay medallion embossed with the face of a lion. Lin's team went on to identify dozens of possible burial sites in the area.

EXPLORING WITH TECHNOLOGY

Lin's explorations are groundbreaking because they never break ground. Computer-based technologies allow him to gather, **synthesize**, and visualize data without disturbing a single blade of grass.

"Exploration has always been about going where we haven't been able to go before," Lin notes. "Environmental, cultural, or political obstacles may have prevented us from exploring certain places. Today technology helps us navigate past those old barriers." For Lin, tools such as satellite imagery, ground-penetrating radar, and remote **sensors** permit him to make archaeological discoveries while respecting the land and beliefs of **indigenous** people.

"It's all about using technologies in ways they weren't originally intended," explains Lin. "We can apply tools that were created for entirely different fields to search for something else—in my case, archaeological artifacts. I'm building on the work of many pioneers."

When Lin and his team return to the Forbidden Zone, they will examine the possible

TECHNOLOGY WALL
Lin and team members examine images on the HIPerSpace (Highly Interactive Parallelized Display Space) wall at the University of California—the world's highest resolution display system. It gives researchers detailed images never before possible.

burial sites thoroughly. Instead of digging, the team will probe them with the tools that allow them to see what's under the surface. Most Mongolians consider Genghis Khan the greatest military commander of all time and also a great spiritual leader. Many Mongolians believe any disturbance of his tomb could trigger a curse that would end the world.

"Using traditional archaeological methods would be disrespectful to believers," Lin says. "The ability to explore in a **noninvasive** way lets us try to solve this ancient secret without overstepping cultural barriers. It also allows us to empower Mongolian researchers with tools they might not have access to otherwise. By locating his tomb, we hope to emphasize how important it is for the world to protect such cultural heritage treasures."

"There are many ways to look under the ground without having to touch it," Lin observes. Thermal-imaging systems show what lies below by detecting heat signals from Earth. Magnetometry uses Earth's magnetic field to pinpoint underground clues as small as bacteria in decaying wood. Ground-penetrating radar bounces back images showing buried objects. Tiny remote wireless sensors collect data from places no human can go.

"These new approaches could benefit all kinds of projects, from gaining a whole new view of regions like Mongolia to tracking animal migrations to mapping the brain," notes Lin. "The real trick is synthesizing the information we collect into something that can be understood. My colleagues and I use visualization techniques to sort, relate, and crosslink billions of individual data bits. We program it all into a file that allows us to re-render it into a digital 3-D world."

To enter the Forbidden Zone—not the real place but a virtual re-creation—Lin and his colleagues can open the door to the StarCAVE.

VIRTUAL EXPLORATION

The StarCAVE is a virtual reality room where scientists and historians can navigate, fly, and feel their way through landscapes. Backlit screens project images on the ground, walls, and every surface. Special eyewear creates the 3-D effect. Virtual explorers zoom over mountains, down

TRADITIONAL HOUSING
Team members built and lived in gers, or yurts, for their housing while on expedition in Mongolia.

slopes. Lin admits, "It's really fun." The sensation of movement is so realistic that handrails had to be installed. "If a mountain is described in an old text, I can go into the room and travel around that region to see if it actually exists." Lin says. If the technology data trail leads to Genghis's tomb, he could rebuild each tiny point of information into a virtual recreation of the discovery.

Thinking about the power of new technology, Lin offers, "Exploration is part of it. But another big aspect is conservation. In many ways technology has created problems for our planet. One of the greatest things we can do is better use these tools to actually give back to the planet—preserving wildlife, cultures, history, and habitats. I think we have to decide why progress is important. Is it just to become faster, better human computers—or to become more human?"

THINK ABOUT IT! ||||||||||||||||||||||||||||||||||

1 **Summarize** What are Lin's goals in his explorations of Mongolia?

2 **Explain** Lin's work is described as "groundbreaking" without breaking ground. Explain how this is true, using evidence from the article.

BACKGROUND & VOCABULARY

artifact *n.* (AHR-tih-fakt) an object made by humans from a past culture

indigenous *adj.* (ihn-DIHJ-uh-nuhs) native to the area in which a person or animal is found

noninvasive *adj.* not disturbing; not causing damage or disruption

pixel *n.* (PIHK-suhl) a tiny digital element that, along with others, forms a picture

sensor *n.* a device that responds to a physical stimulus, such as heat or light, and sends signals back to a control point where the information is used or stored

survey *v.* to view or study as a whole

synthesize *v.* (SIHN-thuh-syz) to combine parts, elements, or ideas into a whole

virtually *adv.* (VUR-choo-uh-lee) here, using an artificial environment to create an effect that mimics reality

StarCAVE: A Virtual World

Picture Albert Lin, standing in his StarCAVE, searching for the tomb of Genghis Khan. Picture the world around him. The wilderness stretches away in all directions. Picture him stooping to inspect some rocks near his feet. The rocks form a tidy rectangle, a rectangle that stands out for its orderliness amid the chaos of plant life. Picture him making a note to himself, then turning toward a faraway peak topped by an ancient shrine. Picture him launching himself toward it at several hundred miles an hour.

It's an illusion, of course. The StarCAVE is a five-walled Cave Automated Virtual Environment. It allows its users to immerse themselves in huge three-dimensional projections of computer-generated images, such as high-resolution satellite imagery of northern Mongolia. Lin is examining **pixels**, not rocks, and when he flies away, he's standing still. None of this is real, but it is an invaluable tool for Lin's research.

‹ VIRTUAL EXPLORERS
Valley of the Khans project members stand inside the StarCAVE. The floor has two screens, and each of the five sides has three stacked screens. The top and bottom screens are tilted inward in order to increase the feeling of being completely surrounded.

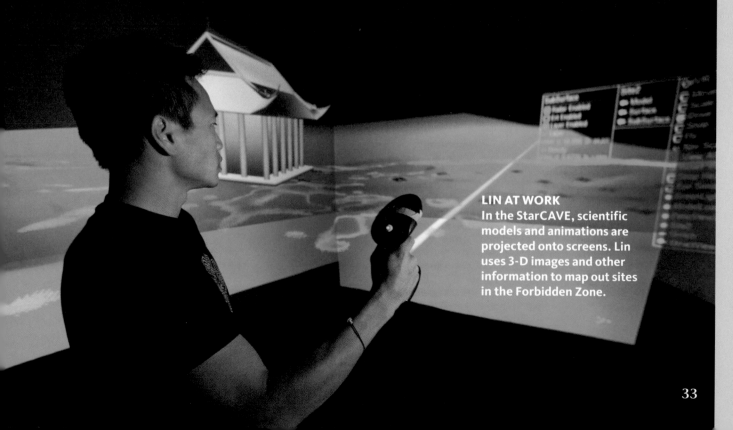

LIN AT WORK
In the StarCAVE, scientific models and animations are projected onto screens. Lin uses 3-D images and other information to map out sites in the Forbidden Zone.

The URBAN CLAN of GENGHIS KHAN

BY DON BELT

Adapted from "The Urban Clan of Genghis Khan," by Don Belt, in *National Geographic,* October 2011

BRIGHT LIGHTS, BIG CITY
Ulaanbaatar's skyline glows with energy by night. The city is at the center of Mongolia's rapidly growing economy.

An influx of Mongolian nomads from the countryside has turned Ulaanbaatar upside down. They are transforming Mongolian society and in turn are being transformed.

A MOVE TO THE CAPITAL

Not long ago a young Mongolian herder named Ochkhuu Genen loaded up a borrowed pickup truck and moved to Ulaanbaatar, Mongolia's **sprawling** capital. Within hours of arriving, he had pitched his ger—the nomad's traditional round dwelling—on a small, fenced plot of bare ground. Thousands of other plots, each with a ger in the middle, jammed together on the slopes overlooking the city. When his ger was ready, Ochkhuu opened the low wooden door for his wife, Norvoo; their baby boy, Ulaka; and their six-year-old daughter, Anuka.

Norvoo put aside her worries long enough to make sure their ger was as cozy as it had been in the countryside: linoleum floor, cast-iron stove, and cots around the edges. Family pictures were neatly pinned to the wall. A small television sat on a wooden table.

Outside their door, however, the view was starkly different from what it had been on the steppe where they had lived. Here, in place of rolling grasslands, there was a seven-foot-high wooden fence a few feet away. And in place of Ochkhuu's livestock—the horses and cattle and sheep—there was only the landlord's dog, barking himself hoarse at the least provocation.

In the **ramshackle** slums, or ger districts, about 60 percent of Ulaanbaatar's 1.2 million people live without paved roads, sanitation, or running water. As in other urban slums, the ger districts are high in crime, poverty, and despair. Many people here do the unthinkable, for a herder: they lock their gates at night.

Ochkhuu and Norvoo weren't in Ulaanbaatar entirely by choice. In the winter of 2009–2010, most of the couple's livestock either froze or starved to death during a devastating period of snow, ice, and bitter cold that lasted more than four months. By the time the weather broke, the couple's herd of 350 animals had been cut to

90. Across Mongolia about 8 million animals—including cows, yaks, camels, horses, goats, and sheep—died that winter.

"After that, I just couldn't see our future in the countryside any more," Ochkhuu said quietly. "So we decided to sell what was left of our herd and make a new life."

They also made the move to improve the lives of their children. Ochkhuu and Norvoo feel no great love for city life, but they see its advantages. In the countryside they were far removed from nurses and schools. In the city they can get free medical care for their infant son, and Anuka can attend a public school.

URBAN LIFE

More than half a million people from the countryside now live in UB, as Mongolians call Ulaanbaatar. Many have been driven from the steppe by bad winters, bad luck, and bad **prospects**. And now that Mongolia's coal, gold, and copper mines are attracting billions in foreign investment, many more seekers have made their way to UB in search of jobs created by the new prosperity.

UB was originally laid out along one main street. Today that road goes by the name Peace Avenue. It's still the only direct way to get from one side of town to the other. From daybreak to nightfall, the road is jammed with traffic.

Add to this a flood of nomads, recently arrived from rural villages. Their skill sets don't include city driving, crossing a busy road, or interacting socially in an urban environment. It's not unusual to be waiting in line and have some gnarled man in herder clothes stomp to the front of the line, shouldering customers out of the way, just to see what the place is selling. If there are other herders in line, they push back just as hard. There are no fights, no hard feelings. That's just the way it goes.

NIGHT ON THE TOWN
Young urban men dressed in jeans and t-shirts
head out for the evening in UB, or Ulaanbaatar.

"These people are completely free," says a well-known Mongolian publisher and historian who goes by the name Baabar. He writes often about Mongolia's national character. "Even if they've been in UB for years, their mentality is still nomadic. They do exactly what they want to do, when they want to do it. Watch people crossing the road. They just lurch out into traffic without batting an eye. It doesn't occur to them to compromise, even with a speeding automobile. We're a nation of rugged individuals, with no regard for rules," Baabar explains.

Early one Saturday morning Ochkhuu, Norvoo, and their children returned to the country to help Norvoo's parents prepare their farm for winter. Ochkhuu helped Norvoo's father, Jaya, cut hay for eight hours. By Sunday night they had moved enough hay to the barn to keep his animals alive through the winter. Jaya too had lost huge numbers of animals during the last disastrous winter. His herd had dropped from more than a thousand to 300 animals. But he was determined to make a comeback, banking on decades of experience as a herder.

Jaya and his wife supported Ochkhuu and Norvoo's decision to relocate. For them, though, moving was out of the question. "I wouldn't last a week in that city," Jaya scowled. "Too much noise, too much jangling and banging. I'd get sick and die."

WORKING IN THE NEW MONGOLIA

Today Mongolia is seeking to reassert itself between the two powers next door, Russia and China. Mongolian **nationalism** is on the rise, and foreigners are increasingly blamed for Mongolia's problems. So are local and national politicians, who are widely considered corrupt.

Visiting Chinese businessmen, accused of enriching themselves at Mongolia's expense, no longer venture out after dark on the streets of the capital. They fear being attacked by young guys in black leather. Genghis Khan is back in style as a symbol of Mongolian pride. Images of Genghis are everywhere, from playing cards to the colossal statue of the conqueror on horseback that faces east toward China.

Genghis is not the only one looking in that direction. Mongolia is sitting on a trillion dollars' worth of coal, copper, and gold, much of it near the Chinese border. There a Canadian mining company is tapping the world's largest undeveloped copper and gold deposit in partnership with an Anglo-Australian company. The Mongolian government holds a 34 percent share of the project, potentially adding billions of dollars to the national economy.

How much of that will end up in the pockets of ordinary people such as Ochkhuu? Experts are urging Mongolia to invest that money in **infrastructure**, training, and growing the economy. The current prime minister, though, took a more direct approach. He pledged to grant every man, woman, and child a payment of about $1,200 from the mining profits.

Ochkhuu doesn't believe he'll ever see that money. In the meantime, he needs to work, and jobs are hard to find. At first he tried to start a business. He and a partner rented a room at a local hotel. They then marketed it to ger dwellers, who lack running water, as a place to take a shower or a bath. Ochkhuu went door-to-door looking for customers. There were very few takers, and he lost a sizable chunk of his savings on the deal.

Now he's thinking of buying a used car and turning it into a taxi. He'd make a pretty good living, and the freedom of being his own boss appeals to him. More important, he'd be able to drive his daughter to and from school.

"We may not be able to raise our animals in UB," he went on. "But it's a good place to raise our children."

Passing through the fence into his yard, Ochkhuu pauses to drag the wooden gate closed behind him.

"I miss my horses," he says.

THINK ABOUT IT! ||||||||||||||||||||||||||||||||

1 Compare and Contrast How is Mongolian life in the capital different from life in the countryside?

2 Form and Support Opinions The economy of Mongolia is changing. Who seems to be benefitting from the new economy, and who seems to be suffering?

3 Synthesize How would you describe the traditional "Mongolian spirit"? In what way does this spirit connect with Genghis Khan?

BACKGROUND & VOCABULARY

infrastructure n. (IHN-fruh-struhk-chur) the permanent structures that are built for public use such as roads, bridges, railroads, and sewer systems

nationalism n. (NA-shuhn-uhl-ihz-uhm) a feeling of loyalty and pride in one's nation; a desire to promote one's national culture over others

prospect n. an opportunity; a chance of financial rewards

ramshackle adj. (RAM-shak-uhl) in bad condition, falling apart

sprawling adj. (SPRAW-leeng) spread over a wide area in an irregular way

Document-Based Question

Genghis Khan's Mongol army was unlike other armies. Every soldier carried all the food and other supplies he needed for a military campaign. The soldiers also traveled only on horseback. Even their diet set them apart. Chinese soldiers ate a grain-based diet, but Mongols lived on meat and milk products, which made their bones and teeth strong. These unique characteristics helped them conquer the Gobi.

DOCUMENT 1 Secondary Source

Genghis and His Army

Genghis Khan was a brilliant general, and his soldiers were well trained and highly disciplined. Above all, they were prepared for anything. In this excerpt, anthropologist Jack Weatherford describes how Genghis Khan and his army prepared to ride into battle in the Gobi desert.

> Crossing the vast Gobi required extensive preparation. Before the army set out, squads of soldiers went out to check the water sources and to report on grass conditions and weather. A Chinese observer remarked how the advance group scouted out every hill and every spot before the main army arrived. They wanted to know everyone in the area, every resource, and they always sought to have a ready path of retreat should it be needed.

from *Genghis Khan and the Making of the Modern World* by Jack Weatherford, 2004

CONSTRUCTED RESPONSE

1. What did Genghis Khan's soldiers do before they crossed the Gobi desert? Why?

DOCUMENT 2 Secondary Source

Barrier in the Desert

In 2012, National Geographic's *Daily News* reported that researcher William Lindesay had discovered a lost section of the Great Wall of China in the Gobi. The Chinese built the Great Wall over many centuries. Lindesay believes this piece of wall was built around 1160 by the Western Xia dynasty in northwest China to keep out Mongol invaders.

> This northwestern Chinese dynasty isn't known to have contributed to the Great Wall system, but in at least one aspect, a Western Xia origin makes sense. During the Western Xia period, Mongol tribes were rising in strength and making forays [raids] south, ... But, mysteriously, the expedition team found . . . nothing to prove the wall was ever actually manned. . . . "I believe the wall here is only half built and that there was, for some reason, a rethink on locating the wall here," Lindesay said. "It isn't difficult to imagine how the . . . Great Wall segment's harsh desert location might have led to the remote frontier defense being abandoned," he added.

from "'Lost' Great Wall of China Segment Found?" by James Owen, news.nationalgeographic.com, March 19, 2012

CONSTRUCTED RESPONSE

2. According to Lindesay, why wasn't the section of wall ever completed or manned?

How did **Genghis Khan** and his army conquer the **Gobi?**

DOCUMENT 3 Secondary Source
Portrait of Genghis Khan

In this portrait, Genghis Khan wears a long wool robe, pants, a fur hat with earflaps, and thick riding boots. His bow and arrows are strapped to his back, and he carries a spear and mace—a type of club. All the soldiers in his army would have worn similar clothes and carried similar weapons.

CONSTRUCTED RESPONSE

3. How might these clothes and weapons have helped the Mongol army deal with conditions in the Gobi and fight against their enemies?

Portrait of Genghis Khan by Pierre Duflos (1780)

PUT IT TOGETHER

Review Think about your responses to the three questions and what you've learned about Genghis Khan and the Gobi. Consider Genghis's power, organization, and skill and what you've read about the Gobi.

List Main Idea and Details Jot down each document's main idea and details. Remember that a main idea is the subject of a text. Details support and clarify the main idea.

Write Write a topic sentence that answers this question: How did Genghis Khan and his army conquer the Gobi? Then write a paragraph that supports your topic sentence using evidence from the documents.

INDEX

||||||||||||||||||||||||||||||||||||||||||||||||

SKILLS